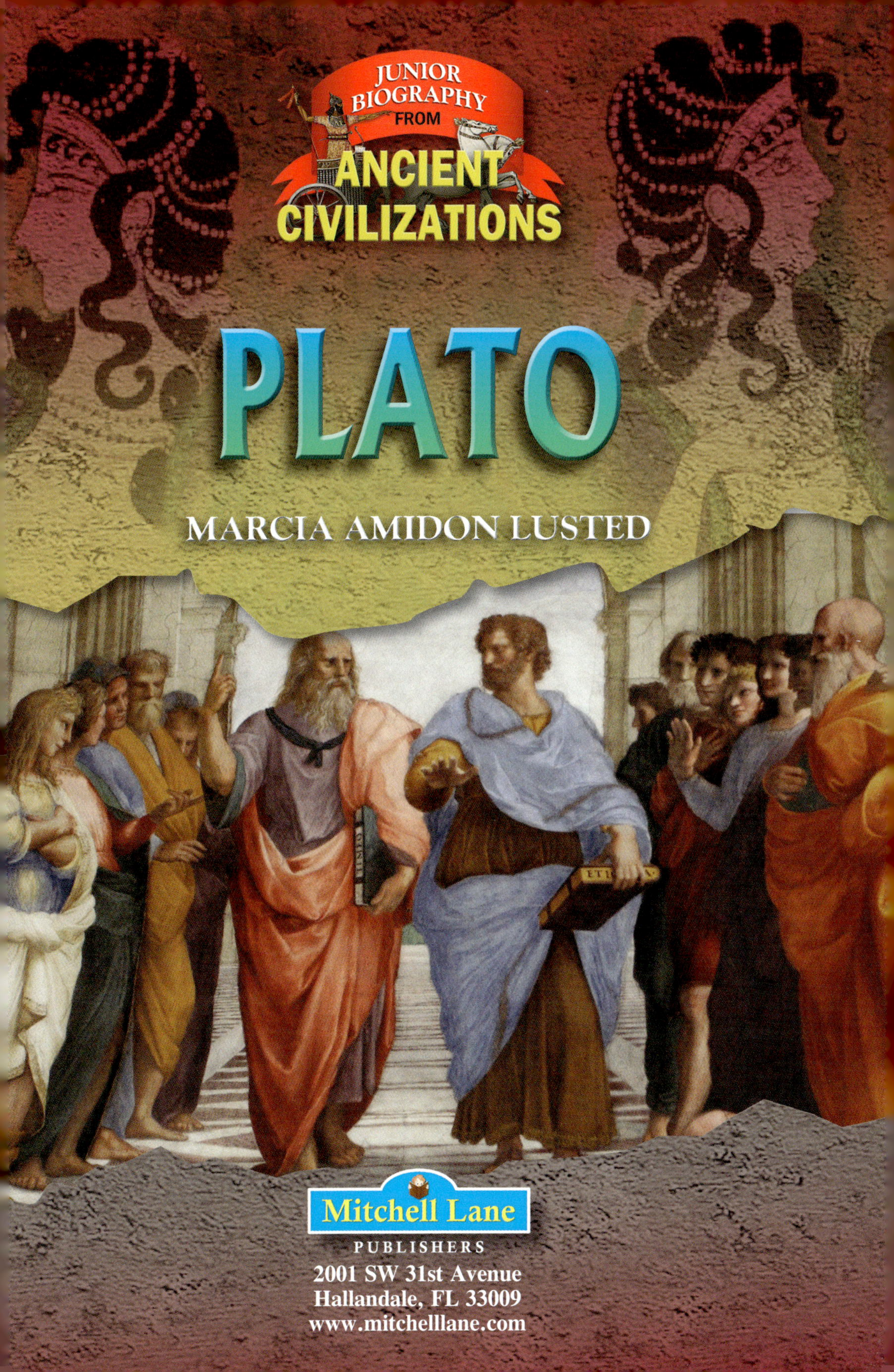
JUNIOR BIOGRAPHY FROM
ANCIENT CIVILIZATIONS
PLATO
MARCIA AMIDON LUSTED
Mitchell Lane
PUBLISHERS
2001 SW 31st Avenue
Hallandale, FL 33009
www.mitchelllane.com

Alexander the Great • Archimedes • Augustus Caesar
Buddha • Charlemagne • Cleopatra • Confucius
Genghis Khan • Hammurabi • Hippocrates • Homer
Julius Caesar • King Arthur • Leif Erikson • Marco Polo
Moses • Nero • Plato • Pythagoras • Socrates

ABOUT THE AUTHOR: Marcia Amidon Lusted has written over 100 books and 500 magazine articles for young readers. She lives in New Hampshire. Visit her at www.adventuresinnonfiction.com for more information about her books.

PUBLISHER'S NOTE: The facts on which the story in this book is based have been thoroughly researched. Documentation of such research can be found on pages 44–45. While every possible effort has been made to ensure accuracy, the publisher will not assume liability for damages caused by inaccuracies in the data, and makes no warranty on the accuracy of the information contained herein.

To reflect current usage, we have chosen to use the secular era designations BCE ("before the common era") and CE ("of the common era") instead of the traditional designations BC ("before Christ") and AD (*anno Domini,* "in the year of the Lord").

Printing 1 2 3 4 5 6 7 8 9

Library of Congress Cataloging-in-Publication Data

Names: Lusted, Marcia Amidon, author.
Title: Plato / by Marsha Amidon Lusted.
Description: Hallandale, FL : Mitchell Lane Publishers, 2018. | Series: Junior biography from ancient civilizations | Includes bibliographical references and index.
Identifiers: LCCN 2017009110 | ISBN 9781680200263 (library bound)
Subjects: LCSH: Plato—Juvenile literature.
Classification: LCC B393 .L87 2017 | DDC 184 —dc23
LC record available at https://lccn.loc.gov/2017009110

eBook ISBN: 978-1-618020-027-0

CONTENTS

Phonetic pronunciations of words in **bold** can be found on page 46.

This portrait of Plato was created by Spanish artist Pedro Berruguete in about 1477. The clothing reflects what was worn during Berruguete's era rather than what Plato would actually have worn.

CHAPTER 1
A Life-Changing Meeting

In about 409 BCE (Before the Common Era), a momentous meeting took place in Athens, Greece. A young Athenian man named **Plato*** met the philosopher and teacher **Socrates**.

Socrates was well-known in Athens because he had an unusual way of teaching, known as the Socratic Method. It consisted of asking a series of questions and carefully thinking about the answers. Socrates found that this method worked better than giving lectures or having his students read books. It helped them approach the truth about deeper philosophical questions. By carefully examining their answers, Socrates could help them understand ideas and how they applied in their own lives.

However, Socrates' ideas and methods did not always make him popular with the citizens of Athens. He described himself as a gadfly, an annoying insect that stings horses and other livestock. As philosophy professor Roslyn Weiss points out, "Socrates, as gadfly, awakens his city by admonishing the Athenian people privately and one at a time for caring about money,

*For pronunciations of words in **bold**, see page 46.

reputation, and honor rather than about prudence, truth, and the best state of their souls."[1] Many Athenians resented those admonishments.

Plato—who probably would have been in his late teens at the time of their meeting—decided that Socrates would be his teacher. Socrates taught Plato the basic elements of philosophy. He also

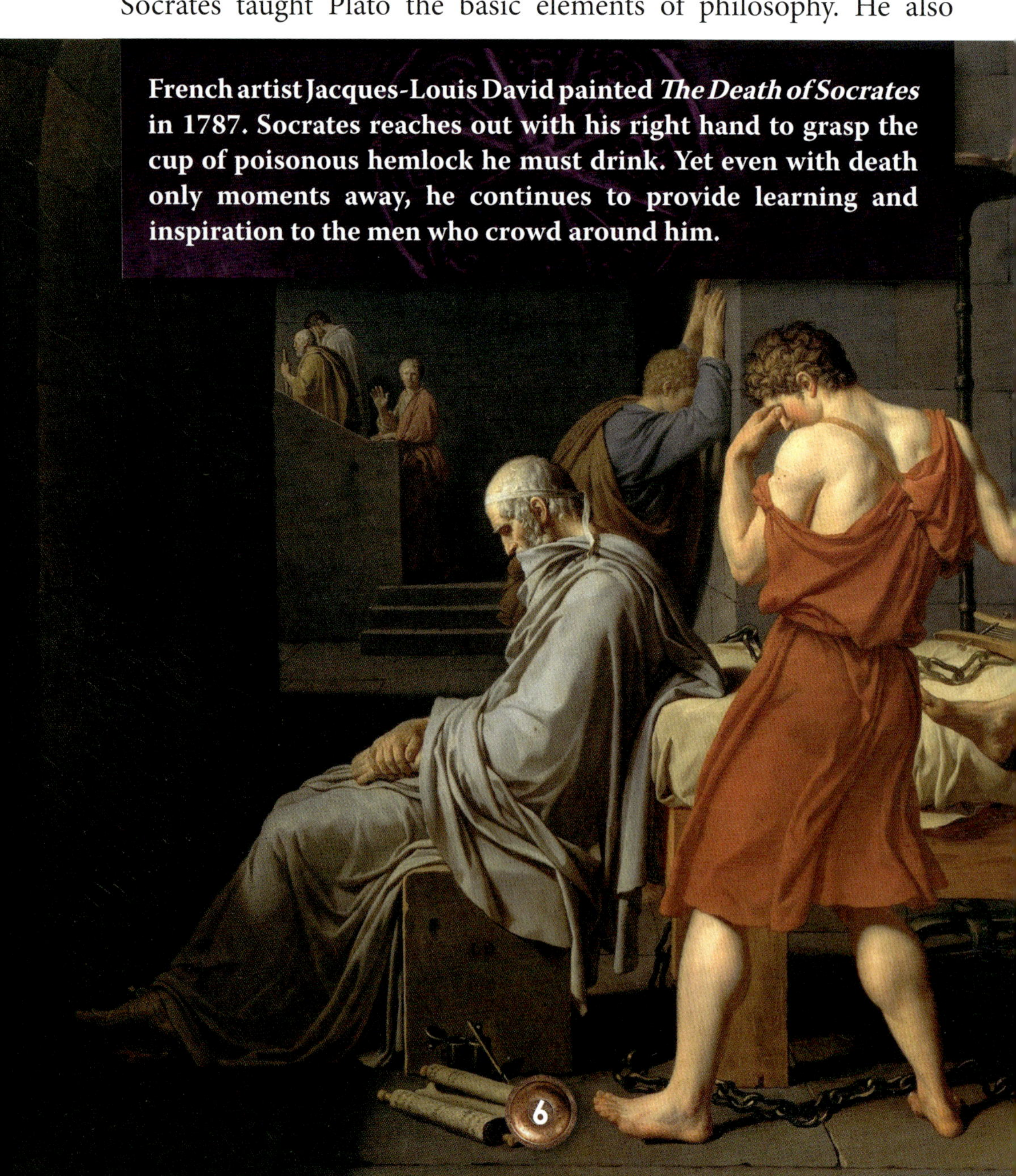

French artist Jacques-Louis David painted *The Death of Socrates* in 1787. Socrates reaches out with his right hand to grasp the cup of poisonous hemlock he must drink. Yet even with death only moments away, he continues to provide learning and inspiration to the men who crowd around him.

helped Plato become interested in the idea of what makes human beings good and virtuous. Socrates wanted to understand how they could achieve a noble character.

Unfortunately, Plato would have to witness the trial and execution of Socrates in 399. A new democratic government in Athens charged Socrates with corrupting the city's young people. They also accused

him of rebelling against the gods whom the Greeks believed controlled every element of life. It didn't help that Socrates had criticized the new democracy and sometimes made its leaders look foolish.

During his trial, Socrates said that he would not change his ways. That statement sealed his fate. He was convicted and sentenced to death. Before the sentence could be carried out, Socrates had a chance to escape from prison and avoid punishment. But he refused. Under Athenian law, he had to drink a cup of poisonous hemlock. He died in his jail cell.

Dealing with Socrates' death was very difficult for Plato. Socrates had shaped Plato's thinking and taught him about philosophy.

Losing Socrates wasn't the only source of difficulty for Plato. He lived at a time when Athens and many of the other city-states of Greece had been weakened as a result of the Peloponnesian War.

Plato was born and grew up in this atmosphere. His experiences with politics, the death of Socrates, and his own ideas about what makes people noble and virtuous would be influenced as a result of Athens' struggles. In turn, many of his ideas would affect the way that the modern world thinks. More than 450 years after Plato's death, the Greek biographer **Plutarch** would say of him, "Plato is philosophy and philosophy is Plato."[2]

So who is this man whose words and thoughts would have such a lasting impact?

Bust of Plutarch

The Peloponnesian War

The Peloponnesian War took place from 431 to 404 BCE. Athens and Sparta, the two most powerful city-states in ancient Greece, were the primary combatants. Nearly every other Greek city-state was loyal to either Athens or Sparta, so the war involved almost the entire Greek world.

When the conflict began, many of the people who lived in the countryside around Athens fled to the city for safety. There was not enough food, water, or housing for them all. Even worse, a horrific plague broke out in 430. Thousands of people died from the sickness. Many more were killed in battles during the following years.

Athens suffered a catastrophe in 413 BCE. An Athenian invasion of Syracuse on the island of Sicily that began two years earlier ended in the loss of the entire force. Thousands of men were killed. The survivors were forced into conditions of brutal slavery in which nearly all died.

Somehow Athens continued the struggle for nearly a decade, before finally surrendering. Athens would never again be as strong nor the center of culture and learning it had been.

Solon was born around 638 BCE and died about 80 years later. He tried to reform many aspects of Athenian life. Though most of those reforms failed, many scholars believe he laid the foundation for the city's democracy.

No one is exactly sure when Plato was born, though historians think it was between 429 and 427. He was part of an important family that belonged to the highest class of Athenian society. Plato's ancestors included a king and a famous lawyer, **Solon**. His family had a long history of being involved in politics.

Plato's father was a man named **Ariston**, and **Perictione** was his mother. According to some sources, Plato's birth name was actually **Aristocles**. He was later given the nickname "Platon," which means "broad," and may have referred to the width of his shoulders as he grew up. Other sources maintain that Plato was his name at the time of his birth.

Plato's father died when he was young. His mother married **Pyrilampes**, who was actually her uncle. He was a Greek politician and ambassador to Persia.

Even though Athens was at war, the conflict had little effect on Plato's childhood and schooling. He received the best possible education at a gymnasium, which in ancient Greece was not

This medieval woodcut provides another image of Plato. Like Berruguete's painting, the clothing Plato wears reflects what was worn during the unknown artist's era.

just a place to exercise. Students also learned about music, art, philosophy, and literature. Plato studied the works and ideas of famous Greeks like **Cratylus** (an ancient Athenian philosopher), **Pythagoras** (a philosopher and mathematician), and **Parmenides** (another philosopher). Plato also attended a *palaestra*, another type of school that combined training in wrestling and boxing with the study of ideas. He became a skilled wrestler who may have won some championships in competitions with other Greek city-states.

Parmenides

It's likely that Plato joined the Athenian army at about the same time he met Socrates and served until the end of the war. After the war, he thought he would have a career in politics. The victorious Spartans had replaced the leaders of Athens' democratic government with a group of thirty prominent Athenian men who would run the city-state and create a new constitution and government. Called the Thirty Tyrants, the group was an oligarchy—a small group of people who control a country or government.

Two of the leaders of the Thirty Tyrants were **Charmides**, Plato's uncle, and **Critias**, his great-uncle. But Plato found that the Thirty Tyrants were too violent for him. They executed anyone whom they thought opposed them. They condemned other Athenian citizens out of greed, so they could confiscate their property.[1] Plato did not agree with their actions and left the group.

The Thirty Tyrants were overthrown less than a year later and replaced by a democratic government. Even though Socrates had

CHAPTER 2

Plato's great-uncle Critias often abused his power. Here he orders his troops to capture an Athenian citizen who disagreed with him. The citizen would likely be put to death and Critias would take over his property.

risked death by refusing to support the Thirty Tyrants, he didn't think much of this new government. Its leaders forced him to stand trial. After the death of Socrates, Plato became so disillusioned with politics that he gave up any idea of a political career. "Whereas at first," he wrote afterwards, "I had been full of enthusiasm for public work, now I could only look on and watch everything whirling round me this way and that. . . . In the end I came to the conclusion that all the cities of the present age are badly governed."[2] He decided that politics were not meant for men who had a conscience.[3]

Being a Kid in Ancient Greece

knucklebones

What was it like to be a kid growing up in ancient Greece? Kids then played just like kids today. They had pets, and toys like small wooden figures and dolls with moveable arms and legs. They played games with knucklebones (bones from sheep or pigs) and made balls from bundles of rags or inflated pig bladders. They also had rattles, hoops, yo-yos, and pretend horses.

When they were seven years old, boys went off to school. Typically they walked to school with a slave, who stayed with them to keep an eye on them. Classes were often held outdoors. Boys learned reading, writing, math, poetry, and music. They used a tool called a stylus to write on tablets covered with soft wax. They used an abacus, with beads strung on wires, for math. Training in sports was also very important, both to keep them healthy and to prepare them to be soldiers.[4]

Girls, on the other hand, stayed at home. Many never learned to read or write. Instead, their mothers taught them things like keeping house, cooking, and weaving.

This marble sculpture shows children playing ball games.

Pythagoras was an important Greek philosopher and mathematician. He was born on the island of Samos about 570 BCE. When he was about 40, he founded a school at Croton in modern-day Italy and spent the rest of his life there. He is especially noted for the Pythagorean Theorem, an important element in geometry.

CHAPTER 3
Out in the World

Plato felt disillusioned by the death of his teacher. He left Athens and traveled to Megara, another city-state not far from Athens. But he soon began to fear that any place close to Athens would not be safe for anyone who had been a close associate of Socrates. So Plato decided to travel much further from home. During the next twelve years, he journeyed through Egypt, Italy, and Cyrene, an ancient Greek city in modern-day Libya.

Plato observed the governments of every place he visited. He took note of what seemed to work in these different governments, and where they seemed to fail. These notes and observations, along with his own beliefs and the teachings of Socrates, would form the basis for Plato's writings.

During his travels, Plato was also studying and learning other aspects of life. In Italy, he studied mathematics with followers of the famous mathematician **Pythagoras**. In Egypt, he studied geometry, geology, astronomy, and religion. This knowledge would help him not only personally, but also as a teacher.

While visiting Italy, Plato spent a great deal of time on the nearby island of Sicily. He stayed in the city of Syracuse, where he became a tutor to a man named **Dion**. Dion was the brother-in-law of **Dionysius** I, a tyrant who had conquered several cities in Sicily. He was known for being cruel, suspicious, and vindictive. Plato developed a meaningful friendship with Dion. Many years later when Dionysius I died and his son came into power, Dion asked Plato to tutor the young man as well.

There is a story that Dionysius I became annoyed with Plato at some point during his visit. According to this story, he had Plato kidnapped and sold as a slave. A philosopher named **Anniceris** is said to have purchased Plato's freedom, allowing him to go home to Athens. However, no one is really sure if this story is true.

Plato returned to Athens in 387. He felt that the danger of his association with Socrates was over. Once he was settled, Plato opened a school outside the city walls. Because it was located near a grove of trees sacred to a Greek hero named **Academus**, the school became known as the Academy. This word has carried into modern times as another name for a school, especially one with high standards for learning.

Plato's Academy is often described as the first university in Europe. It was free and open to any student interested in learning about philosophy and scientific research. Surviving records of the Academy even show the names of two women who attended the school, a rarity in an era in which nearly all women had little if any education. Plato saw the Academy as a place where he could teach young people about politics and help them prepare to be responsible adults and good public officials. That way the government of Athens and other city-states would be improved.

Plato was also very interested in mathematics and law, so the Academy became well-known for its ability to teach those subjects. Written above the entrance to the school were the words, "Let no one enter who has not studied geometry."[1]

Plato leans against a column and waits quietly as Dion enthusiastically presents him to Dionysius I, the ruler of Syracuse. The king's expression suggests that he isn't impressed. In fact, he may even have sold Plato into slavery.

These statues of Plato and Socrates are on pedestals in front of the modern-day Academy of Athens. It was founded in 1926 and is the country's most prestigious research institute.

Plato was not the first philosopher to start a school. But many early schools depended on just one person to teach all the students. Plato was more organized. In his Academy, he was the headmaster and supervised other teachers. He even set up a system in which someone else could step in as temporary headmaster if Plato had to leave Athens. He also had a plan for continuing the school after his death, so the Academy could survive without him.

It remained in operation until 529 CE (Common Era). The Roman emperor **Justinian**, who was a Christian, believed the Academy encouraged the growth of pagan ideas and ordered it to be shut down.[2]

mosaic of Justinian I

Plato was the Academy's principal instructor for forty years. His students included men who would become important in the development of Greek culture, such as the philosopher **Aristotle**. Because Plato was famous, and because his students were his devoted followers, many of his works were copied word for word by those students. These works help to show how Plato thought and provide some idea of how he probably taught his students.

The Water Clock

One of the things that Plato learned about during his travels in Egypt was the *clepsydra*, or water clock. This clock measured time by regulating the amount of water that flowed through a narrow opening during a certain period of time. Often the water would drip into columns or containers with markings to show "hours" or some other measurement of time. Clepsydras were especially important for priests, who needed to perform rituals at certain hours of the day or night.

Plato thought that water clocks were very important, so he brought the concept with him when he returned to Athens. He even invented a water alarm clock, though it's not clear exactly how it worked.

According to one explanation, a small vessel containing lead balls floated in a large vat. Water was added to the vat at a steady rate during the night. At about dawn, the vessel would rise to the top of the vat and tip over. The lead balls would clatter into a copper container, waking the sleeper.

Another version suggests that two or more jars were connected with one another. Rising water in one jar forced air out through a thin tube, making a whistling sound as it escaped.[3]

A reconstruction of a clay water clock from the late 5th century BCE.

This scene shows Plato instructing a group of students in the Academy. During good weather, these lessons would normally take place outdoors.

CHAPTER 4
Teaching by Talking

Many historians think Plato began writing when he was young, before meeting Socrates. They believe that at first he wrote tragedies. These were plays that did not end happily and were often based on myths. Plato planned on entering one of his tragedies in a contest. But after hearing Socrates talk, he burned it.

The death of Socrates changed the direction of Plato's writing. "Plato was passionately convinced that Socrates had been right," philosophy professor Robert Sherrick Brumbaugh notes. "Plato did not intend to let the Athenians succeed in silencing Socrates by executing him. He intended to show that Socrates was, as he claimed to be, a public benefactor, not a criminal."[1] Plato began writing what are called dialogues.

In these dialogues, he used conversations between characters to explain his philosophical ideas. The characters argue about a topic by asking each other questions. Usually the first questions are general and the answers are easy.

Then the questions get more difficult and need answers that involve more serious and abstract thought.

Because they read more like stories, the dialogues made it easier to understand what he was trying to say. By writing this way, Plato could also present several different opinions or points of view on a subject, and the reader could decide which one was valid.[2]

Plato did not make himself a part of the dialogues. Instead, he used real people he knew or imagined characters. Sometimes a dialogue is a conversation being listened to silently by a group of people. Other times a dialogue takes place between two people and no one else is listening to them.

Historians often divide Plato's Dialogues into three groups, which correspond to the time periods in which they were written. The first group is called the Socratic dialogues, because Plato is staying very close to the teachings of Socrates and the ideas he is presenting. These dialogues were probably written during the years after Plato fled from Athens and was traveling. They feature Socrates himself as the central character, talking about his own views. Plato may have been trying to make sure that Socrates' teachings were preserved by writing them down.

Three of the most famous dialogues in the Socratic group are the *Euthyphro*, the *Apology*, and the *Crito*. The *Euthyphro* discusses the days before Socrates's trial. The *Apology* focuses on Socrates' defense against the charges that he was corrupting the youth of Athens. While the word "apology" today means saying that a person is sorry, its meaning when Plato was writing was defending one's beliefs. The *Crito* deals with Socrates' final days in prison, before he was executed. Plato uses these events and settings to explore questions about the Greek gods, whether or not laws should be sacred, and if a person's soul is immortal.[3]

The second group of Plato's dialogues is called the Middle, or Transformation Period. In these writings, Plato is beginning to find his own voice instead of just explaining Socrates' ideas. Socrates is

Teaching by Talking

Plato developed a way of teaching using a series of dialogues. Sometimes the dialogues were set in the home of a wealthy person. The characters would discuss philosophical ideas while enjoying food, wine, and musical entertainment.

often still a character in these dialogues. But Plato begins talking about bigger philosophical themes in these writings, such as whether or not people can be taught how to be virtuous.

The most famous dialogue of this middle group is the *Republic*. It talks about all the elements of an ideal state. These include religion, the arts, education, ethics, and many more. It discusses the different types of governments and ends with a description of what Plato believed was the best. The only people who could be good rulers were philosopher-kings.[4] They had to undergo many years of rigorous training and learning before they were capable of ruling. Because only a handful could receive this training and learning, Plato was opposed to democracy. He didn't believe that most people were capable of the type of knowledge that would enable them to make wise decisions. One of the most important ideas Plato explores in the *Republic* is his belief that the world of ideas is constant and true, while the world we experience through our human senses is deceptive and changeable.[5]

Another noted dialogue from this period is the *Phaedo*, which completes the story of the death of Socrates begun by the three dialogues from the Socratic group. The central character is **Phaedo**, one of Socrates' former students. He was present during Socrates' last hours and describes the manner of his death to a philosopher named **Echecrates**. Phaedo is undoubtedly speaking Plato's own thoughts in the dialogue's final sentence: "Such was the end, Echecrates, of our friend; concerning whom I may truly say, that of all the men of his time whom I have known, he was the wisest and justest and best."[6]

Plato's third group of dialogues, called the later dialogues, were written during the final years of his life. Many historians believe that he made a trip to Syracuse in 367 when his former student Dion invited him to tutor the new ruler, Dionysius II. Plato thought that it would be an opportunity to put his political theories into effect, by making him into a philosopher-king. Unfortunately Dionysius II did not have a strong character. Along with the bitter political struggles taking place in Syracuse, his personal flaws made Plato realize that his plan could not be successful. After a war broke out two years later, Plato returned home. Dion persuaded him to return to Syracuse in 362. But when Plato arrived, he found the situation there to be so unpleasant that he left almost immediately. He came back to Athens and his Academy and would never leave again.

In these last dialogues, Socrates plays a minor role. Plato looks at his earlier ideas about subjects like immortality, as well as the philosophy of topics like mathematics, politics and religion.

Plato's Dialogues would be his legacy to the world. In them, he not only made sure that the ideas of his teacher and mentor, Socrates, would not be forgotten, but also explained his own philosophy of people, government, and ideas.

Lady Jane Grey was a young English noblewoman who was a great-granddaughter of King Henry VIII. She became Queen of England on July 10, 1553 and was overthrown nine days later. She was executed the following February. She loved learning, and in this scene reads Plato's *Phaedo* to visiting scholar Roger Ascham.

In his *Republic*, Plato compares mankind to prisoners in a cave who see only the shadows of reality. He further compares them to philosophers who are able to view reality itself.

The Dark Cave

In the *Republic*, Plato uses a myth to help explain his theories about the world of ideas as being the true world, and the world we see through our senses being deceptive.

Plato asks the reader to imagine a dark cave. People are being held prisoner inside the cave, chained down, and allowed only to face the wall directly in front of them. Behind them is a second wall, and objects can pass across this wall. A huge, constantly burning fire lies behind the second wall. The light from this fire casts a shadow of each object that passes across the second wall. These shadows show up on the wall the prisoners face.

The prisoners think that the shadows of the objects are real. But if one of the prisoners escaped from the cave, he would see the real objects instead of the shadows.

What would happen if that escaped prisoner went back inside and tried to convince the others to come see what he had seen? Would they believe him, and leave the only world in the cave that they had ever known? Or would they think he was crazy and refuse to leave? Because Plato believed that a person's main responsibilities were to the city-state he lived in, he felt it was the duty of the prisoner who had escaped to become a leader for the others.[7]

Plato's Allegory of the Dark Cave.

This statue of Plato is at the Joachimsthalsches Gymnasium near Berlin, Germany. The school dates back to the 17th century. Plans are currently underway to establish an international boarding school at the site.

CHAPTER 5
A Lasting Legacy

There are not many people who are still remembered two thousand years after their death. Plato, however, is still known for the ideas he presented in his Dialogues. He is also remembered as a student of Socrates and for one of his own students who would become equally famous—Aristotle.

Some of Plato's most important ideas had to do with government. He spent most of his life trying to define the ideal city-state, and how to create it. In the *Republic*, Plato wrote, "Until philosophers are kings or kings are philosophers and until political greatness and wisdom are as one with all else standing aside, no city-state will be free of evil."[1]

Plato's experiences in Syracuse appear in his dialogue *Laws*. He talks about how the events there changed his view about politics. He believed that the best city-state would be one where everyone in a community shared everything and most property was owned in common. He would give every citizen a plot of land equal in value to everyone else's. This land could never be taken

Plato meditating on immortality before a statue of Socrates, about 400 BCE.

Italian artist Mattia Preti created this painting, *Plato and Diogenes*, about 1690. The scholarly Plato is shown dressed in a fine fur coat, displaying one of his texts, while Diogenes holds a lamp in the darkness and points to Plato. In real life, Diogenes frequently criticized Plato and embarrassed him in public as often as he could.

away or transferred to another person. It would provide each citizen with the basic necessities of life, like growing food. And because no one had property that was worth more than anyone else's, there would be no jealousy.

Plato's ideas about education would also be one of his legacies. He felt that a city-state would only be successful if its citizens, and especially its leaders, were educated. The way he organized and ran his Academy, and what he thought made someone an educated citizen, have influenced how people think about education even today.

Speusippus

Plato ended his life where he was happiest, teaching his students at his Academy and writing. He was in his early 80s when he died, perhaps in 348. There are two main versions of the circumstances of his death. Some historians say that he was attending a wedding when he died. Others believe that he passed away peacefully while he was asleep one night. He left the Academy to his nephew, **Speusippus**. He left the world a legacy of ideas that philosophers, scholars, and students all over the world are still reading and talking about today.

Aristotle

Plato (left) and Aristotle (right) in a detail from *The School of Athens*, a fresco by Raphael.

Another reason why Plato is still remembered today is for Aristotle, his most famous student. Born in 384, Aristotle began studying with Plato at his Academy when he was about seventeen. Plato saw right away that Aristotle was unique and had wonderful mental abilities. Plato even called him "the intellect of the school."[2]

Aristotle remained at the Academy until the death of Plato in 347. He left because he did not agree with Plato's nephew, who had taken over the school. By then he had also begun developing his own philosophic beliefs, which differed significantly from Plato's. Aristotle would go on to achieve many things. He was the tutor to Alexander the Great, and he created a school in Athens called the Lyceum.

He is best known as one of the world's greatest thinkers. He wrote hundreds of works on a wide variety of topics. These include biology, physics, politics, ethics, logic, metaphysics, history, literature, and language. Many historians regard Aristotle as the first genuine scientist, who relied on observation of actual events rather than just thinking about them. He was so influential that many of his ideas endured for more than two thousand years.

CHRONOLOGY

BCE

(Note: Because the events of Plato's life are uncertain, all dates are approximate.)

ca. 428	Plato is born in Athens.
ca. 409	Plato meets Socrates and begins military service.
404	Plato's uncle and cousin become members of the Thirty Tyrants.
399	Socrates is placed on trial and executed; Plato leaves Athens and begins writing his Socratic (early) dialogues.
ca. 390	Plato tutors Dion in the city of Syracuse.
387	Plato returns to Athens, where he begins writing the middle dialogues and founds the Academy.
367	Plato travels to Sicily to tutor Dionysius II and returns two years later; Aristotle becomes a student at the Academy.
362	Plato travels to Syracuse again.
360	Plato begins writing his later dialogues.
ca. 347	Plato dies.
529 CE	Plato's Academy is closed by the Roman emperor Justinian.

TIMELINE

BCE	
508	Kleisthenes reforms the Athens code of laws, and establishes a democratic constitution.
479	Greek victory over the invading Persians at the Battle of Plataea ends the Persian threat and begins what is known as the "Golden Age."
ca. 449	Construction begins on the Parthenon temple in Athens.
431	The Peloponnesian War breaks out, pitting Athens and its allies against Sparta and its allies.
404	The Peloponnesian War ends with the defeat of Athens; the Thirty Tyrants establish a new government in the city.
403	The Thirty Tyrants are overthrown and Athens becomes a democracy again.
384	Aristotle is born.
356	Alexander the Great is born.
335	Aristotle founds the Lyceum, a school in Athens that becomes a rival to the Academy.
334	Alexander the Great begins military campaigns in the Middle East and elsewhere that spread Greek culture and learning.
323	Alexander the Great dies.
322	Aristotle dies.
146	Roman forces invade Greece, which becomes a province of Rome.

CHAPTER NOTES

Chapter 1: A Life-Changing Meeting

1. Roslyn Weiss, *Socrates Dissatisfied: An Analysis of Plato's Crito* (Washington, DC: Rowman & Littlefield, 2002), p. 24.
2. Rosalie F. Baker and Charles F. Baker III, *Ancient Greeks: Creating the Classical Tradition* (New York: Oxford University Press, 1997), p. 143.

Chapter 2: A Famous Family

1. N.S. Gill, "The 30 Tyrants After the Peloponnesian War." About.com. http://ancienthistory.about.com/od/peloponnesianwar/p/30tyrants.htm
2. Ibid.
3. Rosalie F. Baker and Charles F. Baker III, *Ancient Greeks: Creating the Classical Tradition* (New York: Oxford University Press, 1997), p. 143.
4. "Ancient Greeks: Growing Up in Greece." BBC Primary History. http://www.bbc.co.uk/schools/primaryhistory/ancient_greeks/growing_up_in_greece/

Chapter 3: Out in the World

1. Rosalie F. Baker and Charles F. Baker III, *Ancient Greeks: Creating the Classical Tradition* (New York: Oxford University Press, 1997), pp. 143-144.
2. Ibid., p. 144.
3. "Business News History of Watches." http://www.joomag.com/magazine/business-news-history-of-watches/85?page=5

Chapter 4: Teaching by Talking

1. Robert Sherrick Brumbaugh, *The Philosophers of Greece* (Albany, NY: State University of New York Press, 1964), p. 136.
2. "Dialogues of Plato," Internet Sacred Texts Archive. http://www.sacred-texts.com/cla/plato/
3. Rosalie F. Baker and Charles F. Baker III, *Ancient Greeks: Creating the Classical Tradition* (New York: Oxford University Press, 1997), p. 145.
4. "Plato—Biography." The European Graduate School. http://www.egs.edu/library/plato/biography/
5. Ibid.
6. Plato, *Phaedo*. Translated by Benjamin Jowett. The Internet Classics Archive. http://classics.mit.edu/Plato/phaedo.html
7. Baker, *Ancient Greeks*, p. 147.

Chapter 5: A Lasting Legacy

1. "The Republic." Internet Classics Archive. http://classics.mit.edu/Plato/republic.6.v.html
2. Mortimer J. Adler, "Aristotle's Ethics." The Great Ideas Online, #92, July 2000. http://www.thegreatideas.org/aww/tgio092.pdf

Books

Gow, Mary. *The Great Philosopher: Plato and His Pursuit of Knowledge*. Berkeley Heights, NJ: Enslow, 2010.

Lim, Jun. *Socrates: The Public Conscience of Golden Age Athens* (The Library of Greek Philosophers). New York: Rosen, 2006.

Newman, Sandra. *Ancient Greece*. New York: Scholastic, 2010.

Pearson, Anne. *Ancient Greece*. New York: DK Publishing, 2007.

Sniderman, Alex. *Plato: The Father of Logic* (The Library of Greek Philosophers). New York: Rosen, 2006.

Whiting, Jim. *The Life and Times of Plat*o (Biography from Ancient Civilizations). Hockessin, DE: 2006.

On the Internet

Kidipede: Ancient Greece/Greek Philosophy
http://www.historyforkids.org/learn/greeks/philosophy/plato.htm

Kids Philosophy Slam: Plato
http://www.philosophyslam.org/plato.html

Ducksters Ancient Greek Philosophers
http://www.ducksters.com/history/ancient_greek_philosophers.php

Plato Biography
http://www.biography.com/people/plato-9442588#awesm=~oHs2l7f5kv7nm1

WORKS CONSULTED

Adler, Mortimer J. "Aristotle's Ethics." The Great Ideas Online, #92, July 2000. http://www.thegreatideas.org/aww/tgio092.pdf

"Ancient Greeks: Growing Up in Greece." BBC Primary History. http://www.bbc.co.uk/schools/primaryhistory/ancient_greeks/growing_up_in_greece/

Baker, Rosalie F. and Charles F. Baker III. *Ancient Greeks: Creating the Classical Tradition*. New York: Oxford University Press, 1997.

Brumbaugh, Robert Sherrick. *The Philosophers of Greece*. Albany, NY: State University of New York Press, 1964.

"Business News History of Watches." http://www.joomag.com/magazine/business-news-history-of-watches/85?page=5

"Dialogues of Plato," Internet Sacred Texts Archive. http://www.sacred-texts.com/cla/plato/

Gill, N.S. "The 30 Tyrants After the Peloponnesian War." About.com. http://ancienthistory.about.com/od/peloponnesianwar/p/30tyrants.htm

"Plato—Biography." The European Graduate School. http://www.egs.edu/library/plato/biography/

Plato. *Phaedo*. Translated by Benjamin Jowett. The Internet Classics Archive. http://classics.mit.edu/Plato/phaedo.html

"The Republic." Internet Classics Archive. http://classics.mit.edu/Plato/republic.6.v.html

Weiss, Roslyn. *Socrates Dissatisfied: An Analysis of Plato's Crito*. Washington, DC: Rowman & Littlefield, 2002.

PHONETIC PRONUNCIATIONS

Academus (aa-kuh-DEE-muss)

Anniceris (aa-nuh-SEHR-iss)

Aristocles (uh-RISS-toe-cleez)

Ariston (uh-RISS-tuhn)

Aristotle (AIR-uhss-tah-tuhl)

Charmides (CAHR-muh-deez)

clepsydras (KLEP-see-druss)

Cratylus (kruh-TIE-luss)

Critias (CREE-tee-uss)

Dion (DYE-awn)

Dionysius (dye-uh-NY-see-uss)

Echecrates (eh-kuh-CRA-teez)

Justinian (juss-TIN-ee-uhn)

Parmenides (par-MEHN-uh-deez)

Perictione (pair-uhk-TIE-uh-nee)

Phaedo (FEE-doe)

Plato (PLAY-toe)

Plutarch (PLOO-tark)

Pyrilampes (pier-uh-LAM-peez)

Pythagoras (puh-THAH-gore-uss)

Socrates (SAW-kruh-teez)

Solon (SEW-lahn)

Speusippus (spew-SIP-puss)

PHOTO CREDITS: Cover, pp. 1, 13, 16, 39—Raphael/School of Athens/Public domain; p. 4—Pedro Berruguete/Web Art Gallery/Public domain; pp. 6-7—Catharine Lorillard Wolfe Collection, Wolfe Fund, 1931; p. 8—Odysses/cc by-sa 3.0; p. 9—U.S. Military/Public domain; p. 10—Walter Crane/Public domain; p. 12—INTERFOTO/Alamy Stock Photo; p. 14—PRISMA ARCHIVO/Alamy Stock Photo; p. 15 (top) Xocolatl/public domain, (bottom) Campana Collection/Marie-Lan Nguyen/cc by-sa 3.0; p. 19—ART Collection/Alamy Stock Photo; p. 20 (Plato)—Sébastien Bertrand from Paris, France/cc by-sa 2.0, p. 20—(Socrates DIMSFIKAS at Greek Wikipedia/cc by-sa 3.0; pp. 20-21—(background) Hercules Milas/Alamy Stock Photo; p. 22—© José Luiz Bernardes Ribeiro/CC BY-SA 4.0; p. 23—Marsyas/cc by sa 2.5; p. 24—Classic Image/Alamy Stock Photo; p. 27—Anselm Feuerbach/Google Art Project/Public domain; pp. 29, 30—De Luan/Alamy Stock Photo; p. 31—Jan Saenredam/British Museum/Public domain; p. 32—ONAR/cc by-sa 3.0/GNU Free Documentation License; pp. 34-35—Science History Images/Alamy Stock Photo; pp. 36-37—Mattia Preti/Capitoline Museums/Public domain; p. 38—Public domain.

admonishing (add-MAHN-ish-ing)—scolding, criticizing

ambassador (am-BASS-uh-dohr)—a person who acts as the official representative of one country when he or she is in another country

city-state (CIH-tee STATE)—a city and surrounding territory that make up an independent state

confiscate (KON-fih-skate)—having the authority to seize someone's property

culture (KUL-chuhr)—the beliefs, customs, and arts of a particular society

democracy (dem-AH-kra-see)—a form of government in which the people hold the power

ethics (ETH-iks)—rules of behavior based on ideas about what is good or bad

geometry (gee-AHM-uh-tree)—the branch of mathematics that deals with points, lines, angles, and figures in space and how they relate to each other

hemlock (HEM-lock)—a poisonous plant used to make a deadly drink or drug

immortal (ih-MORE-tuhl)—living forever, never decaying or dying

legacy (LEG-uh-see)—something handed down from the past, such as property, money, or ideas

necessities (nuh-SESS-uh-tees)—things essential or required for life, such as food, clothing and shelter

oligarchy (AWL-uh-gahr-kee)—a form of government in which a small group of people rule a country

philosophy (fih-LAH-suh-fee)—the study of knowledge, reality, and existence

physics (FIZ-icks)—the branch of science concerned with matter, energy, motion, and force

plague (PLAYG)—a contagious disease that kills many people

transformation (trans-for-MAY-shun)—a change in form or appearance

tyrant (TIE-ruhnt)—a cruel and oppressive ruler

valid (VAL-id)—fair or reasonable, and accepted according to the law

virtuous (VER-chew-us)—good or pure; having high moral standards